Minimalist Budget

Simple Strategies On How To Save More, Spend
Less, And Curb Spending Temptation
(Without Living On Ramen)

By Zoe McKey

Communication Coach and
Social Development Trainer

zoemckey@gmail.com
www.zoemckey.com

Thank you for choosing my book! I would like to show my appreciation for the trust you gave me by giving **FREE GIFTS** for you!

For more information visit:
www.zoemckey.com

The checklist talks about *5 key elements of building self-confidence* and contains extra actionable worksheets with practice exercises for deeper learning.

Learn how to:

- Solve 80% of you self-esteem issues with one simple change
- Keep your confidence permanent without falling back to self-doubt
- Not fall into the trap of promising words
- Overcome anxiety
- Be confident among other people

The cheat sheet teaches you three key daily routine techniques to become more productive, have less stress in your life, and be more well-balanced. It also has a step-by-step sample sheet that you can fill in with your daily routines.

Discover how to:

- Overcome procrastination following 8 simple steps
- Become more organized
- Design your yearly, monthly, weekly and daily tasks in the most productive way.
- 3 easy tricks to level up your mornings

Table Of Contents

Introduction

I spent all my money on a pair of trousers...

I was sixteen, living alone for two years. I struggled to make a living giving supplementary classes to my fellow students. I didn't have more than a hundred dollars to spend a month, and yet I spent eighty on a pair of jeans. It was a low point of my financial career.

My parents are terrible at budgeting. They once made it, they got lucky with a business they started. But because of money mismanagement it quickly went bankrupt. Financial fiascos followed my life from early childhood and I was surrounded with examples of deterrent money handling.

In my teenage years I worked hard to have some money, but I always ran out of it before the end of the month. I spent it on useless things recklessly. I lived like a queen in the first few days following payday. During the next two weeks I tightened my belt a bit, choosing the cheaper salami and spending my money on necessities. On the last, longest week at the end of the month, I lived like a homeless person – literally on bread and water.

I solemnly swore that next month I would budget my money, I wouldn't go buying things mindlessly and spend only what I needed on necessities. This oath usually lasted until I could fill my belly with good food again, after a long fasting. My brain got washed with calories and I started thinking about my monthly budget as an inexhaustible source again. I must add that my monthly income still didn't reach two hundred dollars then. To an American, this may sound unimaginable, but in Hungary in 2006, a student could make ends meet if she had some basic financial awareness. Well, I didn't.

Regardless of the reasons and motivations that led me to spend like there was no tomorrow, one thing was obvious: I didn't have any clue on how to budget. And I had no one to teach me, either.

Today I earn more and have more savings than my parents and grandparents ever had. I can save sixty percent of my income, and I'm full of innovative ideas how to earn and save even more.

If you are terrible with finances, feel that your salary can never be enough, and know nothing about how to budget, you're not a lost cause. If anyone was a blockhead with finances, that was me. If I could gain financial awareness, anyone can.

In some aspects it is easier for us shopaholics, spendthrifts and compulsive spenders to change. Why? Because we know the dark side. We've been terrified to death of how we'll pay next month's bills. We felt pain saying no to our loved ones when they asked us to buy them something. Our stomachs shrunk to the size of a peanut because of the anxiety we felt after we realized what we had done – again – when we spent thirty percent of our salary the first day.

Stress, fear and anxiety are enough reasons to look for a solution to your budgeting problems. Even if you don't live on the verge of poverty, you can benefit greatly by learning the art of budgeting.

Interestingly, when I started working two jobs after the first year of University, and started making more money, I became stingier. The more money I made the less I wanted to spend. That's when I started my journey in the financial world. I started reading books about money management and budgeting, I bought my first financial planner and started accumulating a minimal amount of savings.

Weirdly, the more savings I had, the more anxious I became. This seems peculiar considering the peace of mind I had when I had zero savings. I had nothing to lose back then. However, when I had a month's salary in my account I started becoming restless. What if I lost it? What if someone stole it? So, what did I do? I spent it all on Black Friday. Boom. Savings gone. Of course, Black Friday was followed by an even blacker Saturday when I realized what I had done. I cried, contemplated, cried again. Ate...

I learned a very important lesson that day: knowing how to save your money in the short term is one thing. Learning how to keep it for the long run is true mastery. Long-term money keeping requires more than pure financial knowledge. You have to get ready mentally to accept growing abundance. Many lottery winners spend all their fortune in a few years. This happens because because of poor money management on one hand, but on the other because they couldn't "grow up" to their new bank account.

Flipping out of the scarcity mindset is the hardest part. Saved money that you don't need every month is not extra money that you should spend on gadgets and useless things. I know how weird it feels to have extra money in your account if you're not used to having any.

Your savings won't disappear from one moment to another either, as I once thought. Unless the economy collapses, and banks are literally absorbed by the earth, those savings will stay where they are. The greatest threat to them is your consumerist mindset. Everything you see, hear, taste, smell or touch pushes you to spend money. We live in a "buy it now" culture.

I've spent my saved money on discounted useless items because I didn't trust my willpower to keep it. As a *homo economicus* with wide knowledge, I rationalized my actions as "I saved myself from spending it on full-priced useless items. How much more I could buy spending it on these cheap useless items?"

The problem with a consumerist mindset is that regardless of how much you make, you'll spend it. If you have two hundred dollars a month, you'll spend it on cheap stuff. If you have twenty grand, you'll spend it on luxury stuff. It's not about the money, really.

It is not enough to learn how to budget your money. You need a total change of mindset to make your saving efforts worthwhile. Otherwise, you'll just spend your savings at the next tempting marketing trap.

This is how I ended up embracing the minimalist lifestyle. Keeping things simple, reducing needs, and surrounding myself only with the loved and cozy necessary things added a lot of value to my budgeting knowledge. The mixture of reasonable, reduced needs and financial awareness is an unbeatable pair when it comes to savings.

Before you get scared and start making excuses about hating numbers and being poor at math, let me tell you this. I hate numbers and math, too. I'm not good with them, therefore I don't like them. This is why I tried to find the easiest, most straightforward budgeting method for myself – and now for you.

In this book you'll find out how to create a budget for yourself, how and why you should choose to be on a minimalist budget, and how your life will benefit by doing so.

Chapter 1- Why Is It Important to Budget?

What Is Budgeting?

According to the *Business Dictionary*, budgeting is "an estimate of costs, revenues, and resources over a specified period, reflecting a reading of future financial conditions and goals." In other words, budgeting is the method of making a plan on how to spend your money. Creating this spending plan helps you foresee whether or not you will have sufficient money to buy the things you need or like.

You can be flexible in doing your own budget. If you don't have enough money one month for non-compulsive expenses, you can use budgeting to prioritize your spending in a way to save some money for the next month and the next. Slowly, by focusing on saving your money to buy the things that are most important to you, you'll actually be able to get them without entering into debt. If your goal, or most desired financial objective, is to have some savings, with the right budgeting you can put five, ten, twenty, or even thirty percent of your income aside in your savings account.

Since budgeting gives you some financial transparency, you can make sure to always have enough money for your needs, and even wishes. If you commit to follow your self-made spending plan, if you made your priorities right, you will keep yourself out of debt. If you already have some debt, slowly but surely you can work your way out of it without accumulating more.

Budgeting, in my opinion, is the most effective anti-stress medication. Some people would rather dig their heads in the sand without following their money flow. They can stay carefree for a while, but as the saying says, death and taxes — and debts - always find you. Staying financially unaware is not a good way of approaching life.

"I don't like to kill my nerves with that filthy money," some say. Not counting the filthy money will eventually kill more nerves than counting it. Even if money by itself doesn't grant happiness, it gives a peace of mind. And having a peace of mind to me is synonymous to happiness.

Also, being financially aware is part of being adult. We live in a world where money matters and money talks. Shortage of money screams. More breakups, heart attacks and mental illness happen because of the stress coming from a lack of financial security than any other stress source. Like it or not, basic money management skill is a crucial part of living in society.

What Is Budget Forecasting and Planning?

When you create your first spending plan and start using it, you'll see how transparent your life becomes. You'll see what you've spent your money on item by item, day by day. If you still want to cut expenses, you will have a clear picture about where can you make these cuts.

When you get familiar with living on your budget, you can try mapping out your finances for three to six months in advance. This is budget planning.

Take into consideration all the income and expenses you'll have in the next few months. Put everything on your budget, month by month. This way you can easily forecast in which months you will need to tighten your budget, and which months are those where you'll have extra money.

For example, in April is your spouse's and child's birthday. This month you'll probably have to save up some extra money for presents. But in March, let's say you have a demand-free month when you don't have to spend on anything, apart from the basic needs, so you can separate some money from that month for April. Briefly, this is budget forecasting.

In most cases expenses month by month aren't linear. You'll need to think ahead, forecast and plan your budget to even out the highs and lows in your finances almost every time. It is just a matter of practice to do it well, and quite quickly you'll be able to manage your life stress free.

Making a budget plan ahead from three to six to twelve months into the future helps you forecast how much money you can realistically save for vacations, high-cost needs (house, car, new laptop), or emergency savings. It is critical to be honest and realistic when you make your plans. If you have a low income, it is not realistic to hope for saving more than fifty percent monthly. You can, however, see clearly that your income in the present won't allow you the lifestyle you want to live, even with tightening your belt and saving like crazy. A budget, therefore, can also reveal you the ugly truth about your finances, and can motivate you to study, improve and change jobs to one with a bigger income. Or, look for alternative money sources like passive income sources.

How Will Budgeting Help Your Life?

Budgeting doesn't only show you how to manage your finances better but, especially in the beginning, highlights your bad spending habits. Luckily, you can't sugarcoat them. Numbers have a good quality – they show the plain facts. Building a budget is the best way to notice which items you don't need, and therefore shouldn't waste money on. I'm not only talking about the orange juice you buy daily at Starbucks next to your coffee, but more hidden things. Things like the biggest cable TV package you subscribed to that has three hundred channels, ninety percent of which you hardly ever watch. Or the thirtieth clutch you just bought. No, they are not basic human rights. With an honest budget you'll see that because of these useless expenses you're forced to buy the cheapest food, or never go on a real vacation. Thanks to the raw reality of your budget you'll be able to rethink your spending habits and set some better financial goals.

Are you fed up with those sleepless nights when you had waking nightmares about how you will make ends meet? Do you often worry about your money in general? It means you don't have control over it. What's more, your money is controlling you. Don't let that happen. Reclaim your peace of mind and control, and divide your money wisely. Knowing where your money goes and focusing it on important needs is the best sleeping pill. As soon as you know what you have, how much you need to spend on compulsory expenditures, and how much you have left for yourself, you'll have a more stress-free life.

If you notice that your salary doesn't cover even the compulsory musts, you know that you need to downsize, or make more money. Usually the first option seems easier. One way or another, you'll have to make steps to fit in your budget, and not enter in the vicious circle of debt, or increase your debt. I talk about this later in the book.

The other benefit you'll have thanks to budgeting is that you'll feel prepared for unexpected life events. These events can be positive, like a pregnancy, or negative, like a car accident. If you have zero savings, the happiness will be overshadowed and the tragedy will feel even more tragic. Emergencies never have good timing, that's for sure, but you can get through them with a much lighter heart if you have a few months' worth of savings.

Where Does Minimalism Fit In Your Budgeting?

What's the first thought you have when you hear the words "minimalist" and "budget" together? It probably isn't any synonym of abundance. Rather poverty, scarcity, and tightened belts, at the very least a skinny budget. Budget airlines are the cheap crappy ones. Minimalists have one teacup and one spoon, two pairs of socks and three pieces of furniture. Discomfort and plainness.

What if I told you that a minimalist budget is actually one of abundance than the picture depicted above? Minimalism isn't about having as few things as possible, but rather having as many things as possible that you truly love.

Chapter 2 - Traps of Minimalism

Minimalism as a lifestyle has been around for centuries. It might have not been called that in the past, but today, *hygge, wabi sabi* and other type of movements have popped up in different parts of the world, adding value to the local cultural zeitgeist. A few years ago, minimalist thoughts and practices invaded the Internet in a big way. Bloggers, high achievers, and their followers post daily about being humble, downsizing their environment and living simple. The "100 Thing Challenge" seems to be the new black.

The Distortion of Minimalism

In this resurrected movement, not only minimalism fans saw a chance but also service providers. Furniture companies, restaurants, interior designers and many others started sticking the word "minimalist" on their products and sell them for a higher price than the regular items. Posh minimalist items can cost us hundreds and thousands of dollars.

Even if you downsize and declutter your home and choose to live with less, that doesn't necessarily mean that you're saving money. You could spend thousands of dollars a month and still fit under the minimalist umbrella. You may only be able to spend on a few, unique "minimalist" items, for example, buying a new, minimalist-designed chest of drawers for five thousand dollars. Regardless of the price, that still counts as one item.

In conventional practice there is no limit to wasting money that still qualifies as minimalism. Long story short, following minimalism as a style of decoration only can lead you to buy items that won't help your budget.

Knowing this, you can be aware of the traps that today's merchandise and sellers have set for you. Becoming a minimalist doesn't mean filling your house with designer objects labeled as minimal.

Don't believe that the more expensive minimalist objects you own, the more minimal you are.

Some people do that: they spend their entire income to live in a minimalist environment. I call them the "fake minimalist". Why? In reality, they are just another type of consumerist. They are the mass consumers of the minimalism myth. If they truly believe that they are living minimally, that's a problem. They live in self-deception, hoping their lives will get better and simpler, but in fact they just entered a different kind of maze of spending.

I don't want to be judgmental. If you can afford to create a minimalist environment for yourself with minimalist items having maximalist costs, good for you. Do it. If you don't have stress on your mind spending your money in such a manner, do it. If your biggest dream, greatest wish is to live in a minimal designer-looking apartment, do it. You won't be saving money with this type of minimalist lifestyle, but you probably aren't aiming for that. In this case, this book won't be helpful for you. Get a home décor book instead. If, however, you recognized yourself as a "fake minimalist" and you'd like to turn this bad spending habit around, keep reading.

What's the right mindset for a minimalist budget? Balancing minimalism and frugality. There is no other way to achieve the following two objectives: a life with less demands and saving money. True minimalism encourages frugality.

Benefits of a Minimalist Mindset

How did I choose to introduce and mix minimalism with my finances?

In my understanding, the definition of minimalism is the mindset that helps you realize what has value in your life now and in the future, so you can let go of what doesn't. This doesn't apply only to physical items, it applies to all the areas of your life: habits, relationships, health, work, and finances.

Minimalism is not about more or less, and therefore you can't be "minimalist enough." It is, rather, a mental crutch that helps you realize what has value in your life. The more values you discover, the easier it becomes to appreciate what you have, add the feeling of gratitude for what you have and for what you're about to let go of and be happy. That's the ultimate goal I want to achieve with minimalism.

Minimalism is not only retrospective, but also futuristic. I can use it to let go of future purchases before I'd even buy them. As soon as I define what has value and what doesn't in my life, I can easily predict in which category do my future wishes fall.

For example, I like the color yellow but it fits me horribly. It's simply not my color. I knew this since the first yellow shirt I bought. However, this knowledge didn't prevent me from buying yellow stuff and never wearing them again, or wearing them while feeling like a dying light bulb attractive to only sick moths. I did a major decluttering of my life last year (you can read about it in *Less Mess Less Stress*), and I selected one entire baggage case of yellow things. It was shocking to calculate how many macaroons could I have bought with the price of those yellow clothes. Since then, I no longer buy anything yellow. Sometimes the temptation is great, but I'm persistent. It's no longer something that adds value to my life and wallet, and I decided I don't need them. Everybody has yellow shirts in their lives in one way or another.

When it comes to minimalism, it is important to search your heart and mind to figure out what do you truly wish to simplify. Ask why you are interested in simplifying the chosen areas of your life. What are the feelings and reasons that lead you to cast your vote for simplicity instead of complexity? Some people consider a life that is complex to be more advanced, better, and well lived. Is this really true? What is the powerful miracle in simple living then?

Living simply doesn't equal living in a dull manner. It means that your life doesn't seem like a impossible puzzle to put together. You no longer live in stress and constant fear, and challenges that grow like mushrooms need an urgent solution. It means that you're in control. When you're in control, everything is simple and ultimately can be deduced to a yes or no decision. Your decision.

When it comes to budgeting, the only thing you need is the ability to decide what you want or need to say yes or no to. Use the power of minimalism, namely figure what things that have a real value for you are. Real values are a definite yes or things that are worth saving for. All the rest is a no or maybe.

Budgeting doesn't only consist of wants. There are the "must have" expenses like bills, taxes, debts and so on that you can't put on the no or maybe list. You therefore have to be mindful with what you spend on apart of these musts. Critical examination is needed for what you buy and how long-term you want to use that item. This might sound counterintuitive to what I've said earlier, but sometimes it's worth spending more on necessities, such as those items you're planning on using long term, like a fridge or washing machine.

Don't fall prey for advertising that suggests you change your oven once every two years. That's just a marketing scam. You don't need a separate barbecue either, however quickly it cooks the meat. The key minimalist takeaway here is to avoid replacing long-time purchases more often than necessary. Also recognize that every new item that you accumulate will take up space. We live in the age where everything makes us crave material goods. Our rationalizing brains are our greatest enemies. They try to convince us why we need that separate barbecue.

"When we go camping, which we do once a year, it will be better to use our own barbecue. True, renting one costs twenty dollars, while buying our own is four hundred. But who knows who used that rented barbecue before? Maybe some psychos who cooked squirrels on it. And had rabies. And the squirrelshad it too. So, we should buy our own barbecue. It will pay for itself in only...twenty years. Totally worth it."

By reflecting on the true meaning of minimalism, you can reevaluate your cravings, and figure out if it will give you true values. Almost certainly you'll find that your excessive wish is not a real need, just a generated craving. If you're self-disciplined and follow your budget, you'll say no to it. Treat minimalism as your proactive conscience, as the good side of the force that keeps you from spending more.

Criticism of the Minimalist Mindset

When I choose to adopt a mindset I'm always curious and fascinated by the counter-opinions about it. When I started becoming a minimalist, I spent a great deal of time researching what the harshest criticisms of this way of living were.

Am I compulsively searching for the negatives? Of course not. But, without knowing the traps and threats one can't adopt a mindset with the best results. Knowing the criticism draws the attention on the possible pitfalls so one can pay attention to not fall in them. Knowing the "dark side" won't deter me from adopting something. I consider my research like a GPS. It warns me of the obstacles (parked cars, traffic, police, speed check) on the road so I know when to bypass before I hit them. Knowing what not to do is just as important as knowing what to do.

For instance, minimalism in its strictest form is for the well-offs. That lifestyle is largely something only rich people can afford to pursue without fear because their wealth provides a feeling of safety. If they downsize and declutter, but in two months they need a discarded item again, they'll just buy it without crushing their budget.

In the most minimal sense all they need is their wallet. When they need something, they'll just flash their cash. No stress. For those, however, who are not that wealthy, the idea of giving away things, downsizing or having duplicates of your possessions seems and is necessary. Hoarding gives them security.

People who once lost everything don't find anything glamorous in giving their precious belongings away. It has a different value for them. Each individual item is a symbol of freedom and proof that hard times are behind them. For people who have a history of needing to decide whether an item is necessary for long-term survival, instead of whether or not it is strictly needed, the concept of downsizing their home might seem ridiculous or insulting.

For people who are confident that they can easily replace the things they part with without affecting their budget, is easy to embrace strict minimalism. It is an act of trust at the end of the day. Trust that everything can get back to normal if the downsized life doesn't deliver the desired outcome. It is easy to see items as clutter when we are sure that throwing them out does not have definitive consequences.

If you want to stick to the spending established in your budget, think twice about what you give away. Think longer term, plan and forecast. Downsize only the amount that is necessary first. Live and budget with those possessions for a few months. Get used to living and spending on less things. Only then start round two in minimizing.

The mistake people make with minimalism is that they do it by the book.

I'm devoted to go and make my voice heard against that flow. Minimalism is not external, it is mostly an internal experience. You can be minimal if you downsize your things just five percent more than you had before. To avoid the trap of giving everything away, then feeling sorry and struggling to squeeze the replacement in your already tight budget, getting frustrated and insecure is not the way to go. Books can give you a direction. Everybody strives to share their best experiences and practice, but this doesn't mean that those exact same actions will work for you.

Also, let's not forget that the biggest minimalist, sworn to simple-living ambassadors were bachelors. Monks, philosophers, thinkers were quite inspiring for their commitment for not caring about possessions and living in the absolute carpe diem. They could live in this lifestyle because they didn't have to feel responsible for anyone but themselves. Even today, the most famous minimalist advocates are mostly unmarried men.

Therefore, my advice is to approach minimalism with a pinch of salt and a lot of critical thinking. I could give seventy percent of my belongings away because I don't want to settle for a couple more years. I just travel from country to country. It is practical for me to save money on airplane tickets by not having checked-in luggage. By the way – budgeting, right? But for someone who has two kids and a two-story home, this solution would result in a catastrophe. Those people can use my methods of selection, for example, but keep much more things than I did.

Briefly, this is all I wanted to share about minimalism in this book. For more minimalist how-to's check out my books, *Less Mess Less Stress* and *Minimalist Makeover*. From this part on I'll focus on how to create the best budget to maximally serve your needs.

Chapter 3 - The Psychology Of Purchasing

The Iowa Gambling Test

This famous research made by the researchers at the University of Iowa was designed to simulate real-life decision-making.

The participants had been shown four decks of cards. They were told that choosing some cards would win them money, and some other cards would lose them money. The aim of the picking was to collect as much money as possible. They didn't know that the first two decks were "bad decks" and would lead to long-term losses, and other two decks were "good decks" which would lead to long-term gains.

Their physiological measurements were registered while they made their choices. The data measurement showed that the participants realized the winning or losing quality of the decks after choosing about forty to fifty cards. They could explain why picking cards from the last two decks was a better idea. But the participants had another mental process measured apart from the previous one.

The participants showed stress responses (higher skin conductivity, more sweat in their palms) after picking only ten cards from the "bad decks". Subconsciously, they foresaw the punishment followed by the bad pick thirty or forty cards before they could logically explain it. Shortly, their subconscious mind figured out the game long before their conscious one.

The human mind doesn't work on rational deliberation only. It is a mish-mash of emotional and rational decisions.

Emotional responses usually are automatic and heuristic-based. Emotional decisions are fueled by intuition. Intuitive responses come naturally and quickly even if there is not enough information to comprehensively jump to a conclusion. These types of decisions are subconsciously made. The vocal manifestation is preceded by biological ones such as sweating, increased heartbeat, skin conductivity and others.

Rational answers, opposed to emotional ones, are conscious. However, they are slow and require effort. Logical and rational responses are much harder to make, and therefore many people automatically rely on their intuitive gut answers in most cases.

When it comes to purchasing decisions, buyers are more inclined to take out their credit cards led by emotional processing. They make a decision based on how they feel about the product, not on whether or not the object in question is needed or worth the price.

Sellers know this and take advantage of it. The biggest magician in selling a feeling is Apple. They sell a perceived status with their products. Objectively thinking, some other competitors sell better quality products for half the price and they give a much better value. But come on, that's not Apple. They are brilliant.

Emotions vs. Rationality

The brain has two sides, a right and a left hemisphere. The right side of the brain is the intuitive, subjective, artistic side. The left is the logical, analytical side. Some tests can show you which part of your brain is the dominant one. Some people take great pride in it. One important fact, however is always missed: there are no black or white cases. Even if one side of your brain is dominant, it doesn't mean that the other one is not affecting your decision-making. This is even more so true when it comes to buying decisions. You're not a 24/7 ROI (return on investment) analyzing machine. You can't make a purchase based on pure logic.

For example, when deciding on buying a car what should people go for based only on logic? One would think of the cheapest and safest option out there, something that takes them from A to B and has the highest security option. Yet, some people still buy a Bugatti. Why? There are safer cars out there, and certainly cheaper ones. Everything that extends from the practical, economical and safety reasoning is emotional decision. The car's color, the status, the horsepower, aerodynamics and shape are all choices made in the right side of the brain. Buying a Bugatti means that your left and right side of the brain cunningly conspired against your purse.

When we buy something due to smart rationalizing, we'll think that our decision to purchasing it is well founded. We'll imagine ourselves with all the perceived benefits that object will give us. We like to fantasize about our gains and benefits followed by the purchase. Sellers know this, and they specialize on stroking your ego with the items they sell to help you make an even more sudden emotionally decision-based purchase. They shortly present and highlight all the benefits you as a buyer will have. They usually use words such as never (look sloppy again), always (be in top shape), the best, the only, the XY product for smart, conscious, stylish people and so on. You'll feel somewhat obliged to buy that product, otherwise you'll feel that you are not smart, conscious, and stylish. The opposite is also true, if you buy this product it will make you feel smart, conscious and stylish.

The catchiest marketing strategies, however, are not focused on future benefits. They state that their product will offer a quick and easy solution to your pain points. Why? It is much easier to recall and relate with a currently disturbing state (your pain point), than to imagine a yet nonexistent future happiness. Stating that someone will no longer suffer is a much more powerful motivation to buy a product. Once a customer has the conviction that the seller understands his or her problems and can fix it, the chances that she'll purchase is much higher.

For example, you're more eager to buy a product that will make your pimples disappear in two days than one that will make your skin look flawless in the future.

Another magic word we as buyers constantly fall prey to is *sale*. Our left brain gets shot down and imprisoned into the deepest hole of our subconscious mind. Seeing the red sign with four letters (which is not love), we go crazy. This little word snaps us from spending approach to saving approach. When something is discounted to half price we start rationalizing from the saving end of the thread. We focus on how much we save by not having to pay full price. "Oh, I saved ten bucks on this shirt," instead of realizing that we spent ten bucks on a shirt we wouldn't have considered buying on full price.

Sales are the best proof of the customer benefit focused approach. They make us believe that we'll make a real deal with the purchase. In the best case at home, we realize that all those discounted objects we just bought would not have been even considered to be bought at full price. Even if we realize this truth, we're still stuck with the products. Namely, because discounted products have another remarkable quality: they are often non-refundable.

Why Was Adam Smith Wrong?

The classic economic theory first presented by John Stuart Mill, followed by thinkers like Adam Smith and David Ricardo, describes consumers and sellers as *homo economicus*. The aim of a consumer is to maximize utility, and as seller to maximize profit. These are their rational economic actors. Early economic theories assumed that people engage in selling or buying only after considering all the relevant information.

In some fields, logical processing in decision-making plays a large role, for example, when buying insurance, choosing a bank or making an investment. When it comes to smaller or bigger everyday needs, emotional, intuitive decisions prevail.

Even though we like to fancy ourselves thinking we're rational creatures who first collect all the information, weigh it, and only then make a smart decision, most of our choices are gut decisions in reality. Sometimes we realize this, sometimes we don't.

We call our gut decisions intuition. Yet what we consider intuition is the result of emotional learning. Our brain memorizes the emotional reactions we gave to certain experiences. When we have the same experience again we attach the stored emotion to it easier. For example, if fire burns you, the next time you get in contact with fire you know how it feels to be burnt, so you'll avoid it. It seems that you are intuitively cautious around fire, but in reality it is a learned fear. Intuition is nothing more and nothing less than the reactions we feel safe to give to a new situation based on emotional memory. Listening to our emotional memory's voice is instinctual, and grants better chance for survival.

Assuming that we can totally overwrite our emotional memory with logic is not only incorrect, but also evolutionally impossible.

Influence Like Dr. Cialdini

Influence: The Psychology of Persuasion by Robert Cialdini is a must-read on my shelf. It helped me to learn how I should present myself on the market, but more importantly taught me how to protect myself from the marketing influence of others. He has been researching and studying why and how people get influenced for more than thirty years. During this time, Dr. Cialdini securely concluded that in most cases people don't understand the factors that affect their behavior.

In the following I will summarize the six persuasion principles presented by Robert Cialdini. These principles are usually used by sellers to influence buyers. I'll approach them from the buyer's perspective as a warning, or awareness-raising tool. Become a more aware consumer by memorizing these principles and questioning your purchases based on them.

The Reciprocity Principle:

When we get something, we almost feel obliged to pay back what we received. The reciprocity principle explains why free gifts are so effective. There is a soap company in Europe whose marketing strategy is to have an attractive girl or boy distributing free soap samples close to the store. The people they can hook with this free gift in most cases listen product features, they try out other samples, and in many cases even buy the products.

To make you feel indebted, sellers don't even have to give an expensive gift. It can just be some information or a small piece of a larger product that you'll be tempted to buy. The secret is that sellers give you something for free to first buy your good will and trust. The rest is history, as the saying says.

The Social Proof:

This principle lays on the tendency of trusting more what's popular, or endorsed by our fellow humans, than those things that are not. For example, laugh tracks in comedy shows, or satisfied customer short story videos on *Top Shop* serve this purpose, Cialdini says.

We are more inclined to buy cooking equipment that is recommended by Gordon Ramsey or a friendly grandmother than one with zero endorsement. If we shop online, we tend to buy stuff that have more customer reviews and a rating of at least four stars instead of buying something with no reviews.

Commitment and Consistency:

The best new customer is an old customer, says the golden truth of marketing. It's much easier to persuade an existing customer to buy another product from a store where he purchased before, and was satisfied, than to bring a new customer in. This is why sellers have a specific strategy of how to keep people hooked to their store after their first purchase. And we, as buyers are also happy to get the thirty percent coupon from the supplier who we trust.

Sellers first earn customer loyalty, and then they make them commit to their product using different strategies. Customers feel automatically drawn to stick with them. Again, I'd bring up Apple as a master in developing customer commitment and consistency. People who are satisfied with their IPhone, for instance, are less likely to change it even if there are better deals on the market.

Customers are rewarded for their loyalty, with things like annual gifts or a higher discount percentage after spending a certain amount in that store. They feel that it's a good deal to stick with that vendor. For example, I recently bought some make up items at a cosmetics company. I got a coupon for ten dollars if I registered on their account. I registered and ordered more stuff online to use the ten dollar coupon. Right after that purchase I got the notification that if I buy products in XY value, I'd instantly get a ten percent discount for all my purchases during the year. If I spend XY+Z, I'd get this percent upgraded to twenty percent and free shipping, and so on and so on.

The Liking Principle:

People are more likely to listen to someone they like, admire, or look up to when it comes to product recommendations. They are also keen to listen to the advice of attractive people rather than average ones, listen to people who are similar to them, and to those who are kind and praising with them.

If a seller compliments something about me, I'm more inclined to buy something additional in that store or leave a tip. Or both. I almost feel obliged to — see the reciprocity principle. A free compliment for my money.

Another personal experience proving the liking principle was my relationship with Costa Coffee. In a movie called *Closer,* starring Natalie Portman, Jude Law, Julia Roberts and Clive Owen, I saw my favorite actors carrying around takeaway coffee from this Costa Coffee Company. Since then I pledged my loyalty to them simply because the actors I liked drank it.

Put your hand on your heart and be honest with yourself. How many times did you buy something just because your favorite star, your best friend or your grandpa said so? Right?

Authority:

People are attracted to authority and they respect it. They are open to follow the lead of experts, geniuses and high achievers. A PhD, or professor title, an expensive suit, or a posh apartment sometimes is enough to convince the unsuspecting customer about expertise.

Headlines like "studies show", "experts proved" and "scientists say" are catchy, attractive and trustworthy. People like to read or gain knowledge from people who seem to know what they are doing.

People are very insecure and uncertain when it comes to decisions they have to make without having any knowledge or emotional memory about it. They eagerly look outside themselves for information and professional guidance to validate their decisions. This is why authority figures have an incredible influence on people who seek advice in their field of expertise.

Scarcity:

People are genuinely attracted to unique or rare items. Purchasing and owning these items makes them feel unique and special, too. In classic economic theory, scarcity relates to supply and demand. Namely, the higher the demand for an item, the more expensive it will get. Why? Because more people want it than how much is purchasable, therefore people are willing to pay a higher price for this product.

In other words, the less there is of something, the more valuable it seems. The more rare a thing is, the more people want it.

In most cases there is no real scarcity, just sellers making us believe it. Once I bought a ticket to San Francisco. It had a reasonable cost and it had a little red label, informing me that there were only three free seats on that plane. I bought the ticket instantly, but curiosity led me back to the airline's page. Guess what? There were still three seats available even after I bought one. There were three seats available a week later, and a day before departure. Good game.

The Psychology of Online Purchases

Market researchers made a study on online purchasing habits. After numerous researches, they concluded that purchasers and non-purchasers on almost each website show the same behavior pattern: the customers who purchase something spend considerably less time on the webpage than those who don't buy anything. The customers who purchased were not so thorough in reading about the product they were about to buy. They didn't scroll down to the details, and were less distracted by the information shared about the product. Those browsers who took the time to read the product description, specification, reviews and other details were less likely to purchase.

To prove their observations, the researchers ran an A/B test comparing an e-commerce page with detailed information, and another one that looked the same, but with the details hidden behind tabs. The result proved their assumptions: the website which had less information sold more products than the one with an abundance of data.

The researchers concluded that exposing too much information next to the product distracted the customer from the desired purpose: buying. They use their cognitive resources on reading and scaling based on what they read. People are genuinely curious, so if there are additional product details they will not allow themselves to miss it.

If you feel that you have a bad shopping urge that would hurt your budget, do the opposite of what marketers want you to do: read the details. Read everything about the product – specification, reviews. Compare them with other, similar products, think about pros and cons. You'll notice that somewhere in the middle of this analysis paralysis, you lost your appetite for binge shopping.

Remember what I said about purchasing decision-making earlier in this chapter? In most cases you do it based on emotions. The exposure to reading other information than the product's price tag will automatically trigger a rational processing in you. This is good. With the rational system resurrected, emotional gut shopping gets more complicated.

Don't fall for the fist product. Unless you have a very clear vision of what you want to buy, conduct a little research. See and weigh the pros and cons of the different options you have. Ask yourself if you really need that discounted manual ventilator or not.

Don't let online ads appeal to your intuitive system. You now know that abundant information distracts you from purchasing. If you know that and I know it, it's sure as taxes that marketers know it, too. They have improved their advertising mechanisms. They try to push your impulse-buy button by triggering your intuitive and emotional response. They try to trick feelings out of you and push behind the actual use of their product.

Always remind yourself that online (or regular) sellers do not want you to be in a rational mode when you enter the store. Advertisements are made to stroke your emotional decision-making side and nudge you to buy.

When you can't say no to a "50 percent off deal", remember what I just said, and think as an anti-advertiser. Look for the weaknesses in the advertising system. Start by positioning yourself as an aware and mindful consumer and research the product, even if it takes a few scrolls and clicks to find the details. Read all the information available about your product.

Caution – if you can't find any details about the item you wish to buy, be careful. Trustworthy stores have all the information you need to know about the product, even in hidden behind bars. Those stores that offer no explanation and description are more likely fishy. At the very least, make an extra Google search about the store in question to make sure you won't pay for nothing.

Chapter 4 - How to Ignore Advertisements

How Do Modern Ads Work?

In order to learn to willfully ignore or undo something, first we have to understand how they work. In the case of ads it is not different. We have to know where the triggers are hidden in marketing strategies. Ignoring in this case means noticing them. Acknowledging that yes, this is it, this is the trap, and then jump over them on purpose.

The traps are not that difficult to notice. They are pushed in our faces, and at the same time they speak to our heart, ego or both.

Let's see an example, like toothpaste commercials. Did you ever see an actor in a toothpaste commercial who had average teeth? If so, please contradict me, because I never did. The people in these ads all have bright, white teeth, and often are depicted as attractive, sexy and socially admired.

Think about a shampoo commercial. When did they advertise any product with someone who has thin and damaged hair? They claim the actor just washed her hair and became as they show it, but in reality five experts worked on her hair for four hours with ten solutions (probably none of them the one being advertised), adding fake hair and so on. Of course, the woman in the commercial with fine hair gets Henry Cavill's attention and winks to the camera from the passenger seat of the Porsche Cabrio before they leave a fancy restaurant. I bought their product, dried my hair, but nobody picked me up, the very least Henry Cavill. And I didn't look so dashing as that woman in the commercial either.

Cosmetics and hair care commercials mostly target women – although they have their equivalents for men, as well. Car commercials, outdoors brands, or finance ads target men in the sense that the main character in the commercial is a handsome man with a flawless smile, stubble, and stylish clothes. *If you use our product you'll get status, you'll get recognition, you'll be respected, even loved,* etc. The common feature in these types of ads is that they touch your ego.

Another example that is not beauty-related could be an ad for green cleaning products. How do they advertise? By frightening you about chemical products harming your kids. Whether it is true or not, they certainly touch a "weakness" in you – the wellbeing of the most important people in your life. These ads touch your emotions, your parental instincts, your sense of justice and so on.

Most of the ads, be it diet food, insurance, car, skin or hair care, makeup, feature celebrity testimonials and "honest" reviews of customers who used these products and achieved "life changing results."

When you saw the magic happening to regular people who seemed so honest and so nice, in your emotional brain the slightest doubt vanishes about the quality of the product. You relate with the commercial characters so much that you can almost see yourself cooking equally appetizing food with the magic pan as the person in the TV, and you'll naturally expect the same smile on your child's face and the passionate kiss from your husband. Regardless what product is advertised, one thing is certain — the ads' environment is staged to impress.

Key Trap To Pay Attention To: Question what you see in the ads. Try to recall any situation around you when anybody lived such a happy life as in that home décor ad, or was so attractive as in the shampoo commercial. They are not real. Notice how the positive effects of the product are distortedly highlighted. Advertisers hate you, disrespect you and only want your money. They laugh in your face when they present you that overly polished person you wish to become. I used to work in a marketing section as a translator. Do you know what they said in private? "Let's give the idiots something they can't refuse." Yeah, those are us, the consumers. I don't want to put them into a bad light, that's their job. My mission here is to open up *your* eyes and save *you* money.

While I was doing my research on modern advertising techniques, it hit me to dig out the mastermind behind all this was. Someone had to invent these strategies first. Who's responsible for the accelerated mass-sellout of consumerism?

The History of the Psychology of Modern Ad Development

Harlow Gale was the first psychologist who worked in advertising, dating back to the 19th century. In 1895, this good man sent a questionnaire to two hundred businesses in Minnesota, asking questions about their views and practices on advertising.

Gale's main goal was to learn how people processed ads from the first look until the purchase (if they purchased). The study was not a breakthrough success, since less than ten percent of the businesses took the time to fill and return the questionnaire. Even if Gale's try resulted in failure, later advertising firms realized the benefits of working together with psychologists. This takes us to our next relevant figure in advertising history.

The common advertising ploys can be tracked back to the founder of behaviorism in the United

States, John B. Watson. Shortly after getting fired from his academic post due to his scandalous personal (love) life, he got hired to one of the biggest advertising agencies in New York City, J. Walter Thompson.

Watson believed that there were three innate emotions that, if triggered, can make the advertising effective. These emotions are: love, fear and rage.

In *From Séance to Science: A History of the Profession of Psychology in America* by Ludy Benjamin and David Baker, Watson's "...ads sold toothpaste, not because of its dental hygiene benefits, but because whiter teeth would presumably increase an individual's sex appeal" (p. 121).

Even if ads target emotions, the background market research is based on very objective, rational and scientific data. Watson used "demographic data to target certain consumers" (*A History of Modern Psychology*, C. James Goodwin, p. 316). Also, Watson was the first who heavily encouraged the use of celebrity endorsements.

A least well-known but significant figure in modern ads development was Walter Dill Scott. He wrote a book on advertising in 1903 called *The Theory and Practice of Advertising*. Scott stated that humankind is more a "creature of suggestion" than a "reasoning animal." In other words, people are more inclined to listen to suggestions than their own reasoning.

Scott's two ultimate advertising techniques involved commands and coupons. Commands meant giving a direct command to the customer like "buy this here and now", or "use/don't use this and that product". Coupons meant giving a coupon to the customer to fill and mail it into the company for discounts and purchase benefits. Scott was a critical figure in ads psychology development, even tough his techniques were not supported by scientific evidence.

Harry Hollingworth, another important figure in advertising psychology development, believed that a good ad had to have four things: attract attention, focus the attention onto the main message, make customers remember the message, and wake a desire to purchase. Hollingworth was big on testing his ideas. He wanted to focus and emphasize those parts of an ad that were the most effective (meaning sold the most products).

Key Trap To Pay Attention To: Pay attention on your emotions. Observe what emotions the ads you see trigger in you. Listen to your reasoning regarding the thing you're about to purchase. If your reasoning is based on the suggestions you heard in the ad, catch yourself and rethink it. For example, "I need this because it will make my tooth bright and I'll attract more attention," is something you think because you saw it in the ad. You just acted as a "creature of suggestion" instead of a "reasoning animal." Go back to your right mind and do a little research on the ingredients of the product. You should be able to find this online. Are those ingredients really turning your smile into a white, Hollywood one? Ask your dentist, get real. The actors smiling in commercials had thousands of dollars worth of dental work.

What Do Ads Target Today?

In my grandfather's time (1930-40s), owning a car was a luxury. In the village where my grandparents lived there were only three cars – one was owned by my grandpa. A car was considered a lifetime purchase. They bought the car with the thought to pass it to the generations to come.

In my dad's time (1960-70s), cars were more common items. Every family had one car, which in some aspects served as a symbol of status. Wealthier people had nicer cars, and poorer families had a standard car or none at all. Nobody thought about cars as heritage items anymore, but they still used the car until it broke down so badly that a new one was needed.

Starting from the '90s, however, the car ownership model started to change and accelerate. Now, most people consider a car as a tool to use for two or three years, then sell it and upgrade for a better and newer car. Not only the frequency of changing cars , but also the number of cars in a family. In a friend of mine's family everybody has a car: the father, the mother, the brother and her. *"Because we may not go to the same place all the time. We need freedom of movement."* They might not represent the overall car amount per family in the US, but in families who are a bit better off than the very poor, there are at least two cars.

Starting from the early period of modern advertising, we can separate two types of products: the long-term purchases and the perishables. In the beginning, the first category included a car, house, electronic tools, even jeans and other clothing. The second category consisted of food, lingerie, cosmetics and so on.

Today the advertising companies thrive on the following attempt: *they try to make you look at long-time purchases as perishables.*

Compared to the 1940s, when a car was a lifetime purchase, today it is looked at as an expensive perishable. Advertisers brainwash you with well-grounded reasons (safety, speed, reliability, style etc.) why it is worth to give away your old car, lose a lot of money on it and take a new mortgage to pay for this new car. The same goes on in the telecommunication, electronics, and real estate markets.

Key Trap To Pay Attention To: Realize what is a real perishable item and what is a long-term purchase. Don't buy the fairy dust. If you want to budget and save real money, don't try to do it on three-dollar coffees. Do it by skipping the yearly cell-phone upgrade, or the frequent car or home changes (unless you do it for taxation reasons).

How do you ignore online ads?

First, stay offline. Surely this advice is one I wouldn't give a penny for, either. However it is truly a sure way to ignore online ads.

Another method is if you avoid subscribing, or if you already did, unsubscribe from different retailers' newsletters. I started decluttering my e-mails some time ago and still get more than forty e-mails a day. What can I say? Fifteen years, the age of my Gmail account, is a long time and I gathered a lot of mess.

The third way to ignore online ads is to use the app called AdBlock. This smart little application can save you from many unwanted pop-ups and annoyances. Update your browser when a new version comes out. Ad blockers work the best that way. This website will tell you step-by-step how to make the best use of your ad blocking extension: http://www.wikihow.com/Block-Internet-Ads.

Chapter 5 - How to Get Over Compulsive Spending Habits

What is Compulsive Spending?

Have you ever watched the movie *Confessions of a Shopaholic*? It is a sweet, better-than-it-looks rom-com about a young journalist who is addicted to shopping. She is trapped in the maze of credit cards, collecting a debt of more than $16,000. She lives in a constant terror of debt collectors, she doesn't pay her rent for a few months, but she still can't stop shopping.

In the movie it is not mentioned, but she has a compulsive buying disorder (CBD), or oniomania. In practice this means that a person has obsessive shopping habits that bring adverse consequences upon them. Psychologists Kellett and Bolton defined it as "an irresistible—uncontrollable urge, resulting in excessive, expensive and time-consuming retail activity [that is] typically prompted by negative affectivity" and results in "gross social, personal and/or financial difficulties". (Kellett S., Bolton J. V. (2009). "Compulsive buying: A cognitive-behavioural model". Clinical Psychology and Psychotherapy.)

Compulsive buying disorder can be triggered by perfectionism, the desire of perceived acceptance by others, the need for control, or general impulsiveness. However, it can also be a manifestation of identity searching, social position-gaining hopes, or anxiety, low self-confidence or depression. These reasons do not apply to all cases. Not everybody who experiences CBD suffers from depression.

For those who are wealthy, CBD might just seem like an everyday pastime. In many cases it really is. For those who have a tight budget this condition can ruin their lives. Those who need budgeting the most should consider reading more about CBD.

The recent popularity gain of online shopping doesn't help people with CBD, but rather fuels them. They can get lost for hours or days in an online shopping rabbit hole, bringing severe consequences to their work or personal life. Sometimes people with CBD use online shopping as an escape from reality.

The difference between CBD and regular shopping is the compulsive, overwhelming desire to buy and spend against better judgment or known negative consequences. Non-addicted buyers buy for the sake of real need and utility, while compulsive buyers buy for mood-improvement and balancing emotions.

Just like other addictions, buying disorder roots in dissatisfied emotional needs. Since we know by now that ads primarily trigger emotions, it's not hard to imagine how it affects a person who craves satisfying that need. It feels like drugs – it gives a bit of relief when the purchase satisfies the need, but soon the positive effects fade. A new, bigger dose of satisfaction will be needed.

People suffering from CBD think just as intensely and as often about shopping as an alcoholic about the next drink.

Is Compulsive Buying a Mental Health Issue?

We live in a culture where money talks. Better said, objects that you buy with money talk. Everything encourages consumerism and sells the belief that what you drive, wear, or Facebook on actually defines you. Items are the key for happiness and success.

Many people expect social acceptance, self-image, self-worth and self-esteem improvement from their purchases. Buying things for immediate personal gratification is the new black. Overspending our budget, however, can easily get out of control since it is so easy to get credit cards today. People with CBD, however, have a more complex problem than "retail therapy".

As I said before, compulsive buying serves the temporary enhancement of emotional need satisfaction. This emotion-regulation strategy swings between apprehension or anxiety to a temporary feeling of frenzy and positive excitement during the research and purchase of something. This compulsive, vicious buying cycle usually culminates in guilt or remorse. When the realization of how much money one spent on usually useless items overshadows the positive clouds, bitter regret falls on them. The regret soon transforms into anxiety. And guess where they end up "treating" their anxiety? Yes, a shop. The circle starts over again.

The answer to the question "*Is compulsive buying a mental health issue?*" is no. Compulsive spending behavior itself is <u>not</u> a diagnosable mental health condition. It's more a symptom of other psychological issues, like insufficient sense of self-worth or addiction. According to some researchers, CBD is a form of obsessive-compulsive disorder. Others consider it something akin to an impulse control problem where the person seeks short-term gratification while ignoring long-term consequences.

Compulsive spending in most cases results in compulsive hoarding. People who give such great value to inanimate objects have the tendency to feel cumulated satisfaction with the more they have. Hoarding items can also give a false sense of security – I'm closely affected by this problem. This leads, however, to another issue. On one hand, the more things hoarders own, the more secure they feel. On the other, the more they have, the more terrified they become of losing it all.

How to Overcome Compulsive Buying

The easiest and quickest way to overcome compulsive buying is to raise better emotional awareness. The best way is to work with a licensed therapist. An objective, unbiased third party can help you stay on track better than your friends and family. Also, a professional can help you with healthy emotion regulation strategies to understand where your compulsive buying tendencies come from, and overcome the urge of mindless buying in the future. The therapist can help you identify the causes and negative consequences of your actions, and help you figure out replacement actions for the compulsive behavior. It is important to examine the positive and negative sides of the compulsive buying behavior to find an appropriate alternative lifestyle that satisfies needs while being less self-destructive.

There are no specific therapies designed solely to overcome compulsive shopping habits, but there are many forms of therapy that can help people address this issue. Two therapies produce outstanding positive results: cognitive behavioral therapy, and therapies using different mindfulness techniques. The former proves to be the best when used in groups. Two psychologists, Michel Lejoyeux and Aviv Weinstein, conducted research about the efficacy of cognitive behavioral therapy in case of CBD. They highlighted that a proper psychiatric evaluation should precede the therapy to find the most appropriate recovery program for the patient. If the patient receives the most fitting therapy, it will decrease their compulsive buying tendencies after only ten weeks of participation. The latter, the mindfulness technique, therapies resulted in impulse improvement, better emotion management and acceptance.

People with compulsive buying tendencies might want to add financial counseling along with their psychotherapy. Anything can be useful, from self-help books, to online finance and budgeting courses, to group counseling meetings. Raising financial awareness and budgeting improvement techniques can help a lot with facing the financial reality of a person with CBD.

If you feel that you suffer from a milder, or more severe, version of CBD you might want to consult a counselor about it. From a budgeting point of view it is critical to keep your shopping impulses under control. Otherwise, even if you manage to budget and save in the short term, you won't be able to keep it on the long-term.

Chapter 6 - Budgeting Methods

In the previous chapters you read about the obstacles that might sabotage your flawless budgeting plans. It's time to talk about how exactly you can set up your budget and live with it. By now, you know that budgeting means much more than paying your bills on time. It is complex spending and saving forecasting and planning.

In this chapter I will present some of the easy-to-follow and well-designed budgeting methods.

The 50/30/20 Method by Mint

Mint is a very compact personal finance site. You can sign up for free, and if you have an American bank account, you can set it up to track your everyday spending. You can set alerts, track and pay bills, and of course, create an online budget.

Mint's budgeting concept lays on the 50/20/30 rule, or the 50/30/20 budget. The numbers symbolize proportions in your monthly spending. This guideline was created and developed by financial advisórs and money masterminds to help you keep your expenses on track. Regardless of which stage of your life are you in, you can greatly benefit by adopting this budgeting system.

If you're in your mid-twenties, just opening your wings as a self-supporting adult and you bumped into this book, you're very lucky. You have a chance that not many people had when they started their adult life. You can set your financial goals at the very beginning and customize them based on your experience about it.

If you are in your thirties, forties, fifties, or older, don't think you're too late. You can still turn that sinking financial ship around and generate savings and a better life for yourself. Each day spent with reckless spending is a day lost to improve. Improvement starts in the first day. This is why budgeting is so amazing – you don't need long months or years to start benefiting. Better financial conditions begin on the first day. Of course, you'll need years to experience the most fitting methods for yourself, or to accumulate a bigger savings.

Whether you're young or experienced, try your best to include the good habit of budgeting in your everyday life. The more you practice it, the easier and simpler it will become. Feel free to question everything you read in the following budgeting methods. Change them here and there, personalize the core concepts to your own needs. Any type of budgeting system is better than none.

In Mint's 50/30/20 rule, 50 percent stays for essentials, 30 percent for personal expenses, and 20 percent for savings. Shortly, these are the percentages of how you should divide 100 percent of your income.

Spending fifty percent for essentials might seem like a high number at first, but considering that it includes everything from your housing bills to your morning toast, it's actually an accurate percentage.

These are the costs you can't run away from. Everybody pays them in more or less the same percentage. You can always try to reduce essential costs, but they might pop out in a different area. Let's say you live in the city center and you pay expensive rent. However, since everything is close to you, the location might save you on travel costs. It also saves you some time. If you live in the suburbs, your monthly rent might be lower, but the saving adds up on transportation and time.

The most common expenses in the "essentials" category are: food, housing related costs, utility bills, and transportation. I consider phone and internet bills essential than personal expenses in the age we're living in. Feel free to exclude them from your essentials list if you disagree. Some people do.

The personal category is the deal breaker category in your budget. If you choose to live absolutely minimally, you might be able to add all 30 percent to your savings category. In any case, here you can cut the most "useless" spending. Don't feel stressed about feeling the need to spend all 30 percent on your personal needs, that's why this category was created in the first place. Some people have low demands when it comes to "self-defining" costs, and others have higher. If you stay within the percentage given, your budget will still survive. The "something for something" rule applies: if you want more luxury items in your life rather than save more, it's fine. But don't expect an exponential growth in your savings account.

Experts gave 30 percent for personal needs and 20 percent for savings because there are so many non-essentials that people want. If you think that, for you, savings and planning for the future is more important, feel free to switch the percentage of the two categories.

The most common expenses in the "personal" category are: cable TV bills, coffee breaks in a café, makeup, clothing, gym membership, dining out, other memberships... I consider extra luxury choices in your essentials to also be a personal expense. For example, if you rent an apartment in the city center by itself is not a luxury. If you rent the rooftop apartment for better view, with an extra ten percent rental fee, that's a luxury.

These are only the standard expenses in the personal category. You are the one who can decide what is really an essential or a personal expense for you. If you're a body builder, gym membership is essential.

The key feature you should keep in mind regarding the personal category is that the less expenses you have here, the quicker you'll be able to build up savings for a house, car, or to pay down your depts.

The third category in the Mint method is the 20 percent savings. They call it a "get ahead" category. I just nicknamed it your best friend to give you peace of mind. Having savings can grant a feeling of safety. You can be sure that if a car hits you, if you fall ill or just need to a distant relative at the last minute, money won't be a problem.

Some financial gurus suggest putting only 10 percent of your income in savings. Indeed, it is better than no savings at all. Compared to that, 20 percent savings might seem like a daring statement to make. Don't forget, you save for yourself, not for another's sake. The more you save today, the more you'll have tomorrow. Take it like that, if you save 20 percent of your monthly income, in five months you'll have a one-month's salary-worth in your savings account. In a year, two months and so on.

Planning savings into your budget might vary on individual needs. There are two extreme cases: the super rich and the super poor. If you're lucky and inherited two million dollars and put it all in savings, good for you. With two million dollars in your account you could spend all your income on macaroons and still have a decent amount of monthly savings increase on interests. If you have such a low income that you hardly can pay for only your essentials, and you'd risk losing your home if you cut 20 percent for your savings, of course, this is not the right time to think about savings. Think about how to make more money first if you're in that phase of life.

If you're in neither of the two categories above, plan your savings. The best way to estimate how much can you save in reality is after paying off your essentials but not your personal expenses. For example, let's say you want to stick to the 20 percent savings model. After you pay all your essential costs you'll realize that 60 percent of your income is gone. In this case if you'll put aside 20 percent for savings it means you'll have only 20 percent for personal expenses. But if you'd spend your personal expenses first, you wouldn't have just 10 percent for savings. If your goal is to save 20 percent by any means, you'd face a problem and wouldn't be able to comply with your budget. This is why the hierarchy of expenses is:

- essentials
- savings
- personal

The most common expenses in "savings" category are: savings plans, emergency funds, debt payments, retirement savings.

To me it still sounds so foreign and hilarious to even write down the word "retirement". It still seems an eternity away. Not urgent at all. However, if you take the calculation I made above, in a year you can save two months' worth of salary with 20 percent monthly savings. This means you'll be covered for a year after six years of savings. For five years after thirty years of saving... And this is considering that you never touch your savings during those years. There is compounding interest on your fund the older it gets, but still, nobody became a millionaire on retirement fund interest. If you're a young titan, you might not feel the burning urgency of retirement savings, but you'll be grateful at the age of 65.

Developing good budgeting habits sets you on a good track for lifetime. The 50/30/20 method is very easily adoptable since it divides based on proportions, not strict numbers. Everybody who has an income can follow it. As your income grows, the proportions still stay the same, they just mean a bigger number.

The proportions are a framework rather than a rule, though. As I emphasized before, you must know how you can adjust it to serve your financial interest the best. You can always review your self-imposed proportions if you need it or if anything in your finances or goals change.

To me these proportions are somewhat different. I use 40 percent of my income on essential expenses, 40-45 percent on savings, and only 15-20 percent on personal stuff which is mostly coffee. I'm a minimalist, after all.

Educate Yourself

Knowledge is power. Money is power. Power is power. I think I exhausted the most common sayings about power. Let's stick to the first one now. It inevitably leads to the other two.

Personal finance doesn't have to be a mystery. The basics are very easy to learn and require time rather than money. With the online world so opened, you can access the best finance guides for as little as a couple dollars.

I can highly recommend some of the following books:

- *I Will Teach You to Be Rich* by Ramit Sethi (He has a very good course, too. In his work you'll learn much more that budgeting. He delivers what his title promises, the basics of how to make money.) Check out his website: http://www.iwillteachyoutoberich.com

- *The Simple Dollar* by Trant A. Hamm (It is an informative book containing the essential definitions in finance. It is easy to understand and follow. He makes very good points regarding budgeting.) Check out his website: http://www.thesimpledollar.com

- The Five Cent Nickel website offers a variety of up-to-date information about credit cards, savings, frugality, and even banking and retirement. To broaden your finance knowledge this is a good summary site. https://www.fivecentnickel.com/category/saving-investing/

- If you're looking for a way out of the maze of debts, check out the book of Jerrold Mundis, *How to Get Out of Debt, Stay Out of Debt, and Live Prosperously*.

- If you wish to find creative ways to fatten your budget, read *The Complete Tightwad Gazette* by Amy Dacyczyn.

You can always visit your local library or amazon.com to browse between old or new personal finance-related books. I really enjoyed Robert Kiyosaki's books when I was just starting to broaden my financial knowledge. Improving your financial awareness is not a cost, is an investment. Choose the best tools out there to improve.

My Budgeting Method

I love my life to be transparent. Everything I own or do is very transparent – the way I organize my clothes, my makeup, and my budget. Therefore, I use an Excel chart to keep my expenses organized.

As I've mentioned before, I live by the 40-40-20 percent rule rather than 50/30/20. I spend 40 on essentials, 40 on savings and 20 on personal items. But not necessarily. Since my income and expenses fluctuate often, I can't plan with long-term ratios or numbers. In one month I might make X dollars, in the next X-1000 and the next X+1000. I can never know.

My spending is not predictable, either. In the months when I travel I have more personal expenses but less business expenses (which is an essential expense). Even so, during my travelling month I spend somewhat more than when I'm home working like a diligent little ant. Costs also vary based on the country I am currently in. In the US I have a higher food bill at the end of the month than in Romania. Why? While I'm in the US, I can get a pound of apples, a loaf of bread, a pound of chicken meat, some vegetables and rice for ten bucks, but in Romania I can eat like a queen for the same amount for four-five days.

It is chaotic. It took me some time to develop a good budgeting system to keep track of all these crazy changes. If you live a similar lifestyle as I do, this method can be very helpful. If you have a steady cash flow, my method still can be good for you.

As a matter of fact, I don't use Mint's essentials-savings-personal categories. I have six categories based on my most frequent needs:

- Business.

This category includes everything that my business needs – mostly editing costs, audio narrations, reference books, advertising, internet, phone and coffee.

- Entertainment.

This includes cinema tickets (I'm a regular cinema goer), my gym membership, and any other form of entertainment items I consume – books that are non-work related, a night out with friends, games, and so on. It has a strict spending cap.

- Clothes and Makeup.

I don't think this category needs explanation. I try to downsize this category as much as possible, putting some restrictions on it like a spending cap. I also have the unwritten minimalist rule to get rid of something as soon as I get another thing. Within the category, of course. Buying a shirt and throwing out my old cereal box is not the way.

- Food.

Another category that needs no explanation. My only addendum here is that I put a spending cap on this category, too. It usually is 10 percent of my monthly income. In the months when I make more, I eat out more or afford better food. In the months of scarcity I focus on dieting.

- Travel.

Since I travel a lot, to me it makes sense to have a separate category for it. This category doesn't include the riff raff I buy during my travels. Those are divided among the other categories above. It stands strictly for transportation costs. Plane tickets, Uber, taxies, trains, gas price, car rental – these kinds of things.

- Other.

This category stands for literally everything else: housing, paying my University debt, sending some money to needy relatives, medicine, and any kind of spending that I can't sort in any of the categories above.

If I wanted to Mint my categories, Business and Food and some part of the Other category would stay for the essentials. Clothes and Makeup, Entertainment and Travel would be the personal category. Where are the savings, you may wonder? It's easy. Everything that remains by the end of the month goes to my savings account.

My budgeting strategy may contradict the essentials-savings-personal spending hierarchy, but I have strict caps on all of my personal spending and on some of my essentials. I get my money in a 60 days delay, which means that I know 60 days in advance how much I will have two months later. I can forecast and plan my budget far ahead. I literally know on the first day of each month how much I will spend dollar per dollar. How? I know my business expenses based on what I produced that month and I have cap on the other categories. I never overspend them. A little self-discipline and mindfulness is what it takes.

The only category I can't predict entirely is the *Other* category. If I get sick, or something unexpected happens I might have some extra expenses, but luckily it doesn't happen all that often.

Don't get me wrong. I'm not a money mogul. A few years ago I was almost a beggar. I am thankful for those years of scarcity because they taught me how to thrive on a very tight budget. I'm very low maintenance, looking for the best deals and living minimally. This is why I can save so much. My needs didn't grow with my budget.

Many people who experience a positive change in their income (promotion, inheritance, lottery) exponentially increase their demands. Sometimes they don't even realize it. Simply buying the pricier salami and a bigger cable TV plan is enough to make a difference. This is why they have the impression that their money is never enough. If you recognize yourself as a person with similar attitude I suggest you to adopt some of my budgeting method and put a cap on a few categories in your budget. Don't raise the cap's amount when your salary grows. Put the difference in your savings account instead, unless your goal with the raise was to afford yourself a more luxurious lifestyle. That's totally fine, too. Know what you're goal with budgeting is – that's all.

Here's a screenshot about my excel chart:

As you can see I have a Running Balance. I have a box where I add all my earnings, and in the other box my spending. The "Description" stands for the category. Each category has a different color and gets separately calculated. The BALANCE chart shows my current amount of money. Monthly Recurring Expenses is something I don't use anymore, since I have no fixed expenses. For those who do (99% of working humankind) it can be a good guide to collect the essentials there to have a clear picture about how much that is moneywise. TOTAL is the sum of all the Monthly Recurring Expenses.

The second chart shows my first few expenses in the month of January, 2017. The big blackness is to protect my privacy, but to make my point it is not important anyway. As you can see, each category goes by a different color, and in the beginning of each month I put a cap or estimate for each category. At the end of the month I can easily compare my estimates with the actual amount spent. In most cases they match. (If you own a black and white kindle, let me help: Food is green, Business is red, Entertainment is orange, Travel is purple, Clothes is grey and Other is blue. Why? I don't know. I chose colors randomly.)

Chapter 7 - Honey Money

Do you love money? Yes, I really meant to ask this. Some people hate money, they think it derives from Satan himself. Others look at it as a necessary evil. Some constantly blame it.

In my opinion, money as a tool is neutral. It gets powered by the connotations we add to it. It sound weird to say this about such an earthly object as money, but it feels how you feel about it. If you hate it, it will leave you. Who wants to stay with someone who hates it, right? If you love it, cherish it and take care of it (by budgeting and spending it on real value, for instance), money will stay with you and prosper. There is a bizarre power in words, and a weird connection between living and inanimate subjects.

Do you label money with unfriendly attributives? Think about your relationship with money like your romantic relationship or your friendships. If you'd tell your partner or friends the same attributives you tell money, do you think they'd stay with you? (Feel free to answer the question for yourself.)

Taking your relationship with money to a psychological ground, hating money drives you to spend it subconsciously. You don't like it, so you want to get rid of it. How? By spending it. It makes sense. Why would you like to keep, or what's more, multiply something that you hate?

Have you ever thought about your finances from this angle? Did you ever think about fixing your relationship with money?

If not, never mind. It doesn't matter what has happened before, that's in the past. You can't help it, can't change it, so don't waste time on it. Luckily, this is the best moment when you can get started.

How to Improve Your Relationship With Money

First of all, stop fueling hatred towards it. Change the labels you give to money. Remember my example above about looking at it as any good relationship you have in your life. Use those attributes you tell your spouse to money. It might be quite funny in the beginning. This is where the chapter's title comes from. I call my partner "Honey." Honey money. So sweet, right?

The first time I started thinking about how important it is to rewire your emotions towards money was after I read Marie Kondo's book, *The Life Changing Magic of Tidying Up*. In this book, Kondo talks about how important it is to focus on keeping the objects that "spark joy" around you, and to be thankful for what you part from. In her opinion people should genuinely love and respect the objects that serve their wellbeing. Money is the mother of all objects. Everything you own was a trade for money, after all.

Allow the money you have to spark joy in your life. Say thank you for the money you part from. Learn to appreciate the money you have, regardless of the amount. Don't take it for granted. You are lucky to have some and trade it for a roof above your head and for food. It sounds cheesy, but isn't it a much better way to approach money? Or life in general? "Change expectations for appreciation," said Tony Robbins.

Add value to money. Don't spend it easily on things that don't have value to you just for the sake of spending. If you spend your money on things that are not important in your "personal budgeting category" (for example, on stuff to impress others) you'll feel bitter after the purchase. You will feel you overspent, or that the purchase didn't make you happier. You'll feel sorry for the money lost. Even if it was not the money's fault, you'll experience the situation as another painful money-related memory.

Budgeting can improve your relationship with money. At the same time, you need to improve your relationship with money to do good long-term budgeting.

It seems like a catch-22, but in practice it's a self-generating process. Let's say you have a bad relationship with money and you hate it. As a result, you decided to budget. You created a budget, downsizing your expenses to the essentials and personally valuable things. If you spend your money on pure value, the purchases will make you happier and satisfied. If you keep your budgeting on track, you'll start having a small savings.

If you don't work on learning to respect and love money in parallel, sooner than later you'll spend those savings because your subconscious doesn't want to keep something you hate. After the shopping frenzy disappears, you'll realize that you spent all your money, you'll feel devastated, and as mentioned above, attach the bad feelings directly to money.

Now let's see the other side. Let's say by budgeting you consciously learn to cherish and appreciate your money more. Saying thanks every time you can afford something what makes you happy, or takes you closer to your goals will leave you with a positive experience. Respecting your budget will make you proud of yourself. Gathering savings will make you feel secure. Being able to afford your dream home after diligent budgeting will make you feel fulfilled. Your life will be much happier simply because you switched your mentality about money.

Trade Money For Time

Money can get you many things in life, but I think the most important value money can "buy" you is freedom. Put simply, if you save twenty percent of your income each month, that means you bought yourself two months of freedom in a year. There are many variables of why you wouldn't live with this freedom — losing your job, emptying your savings account, but you get the gist.

Think about money as a friend who can give you something no one else can: freedom. The freedom of choice, a sense of independence, and ultimately can buy you time. Time is more scarce and precious than any other asset. Why? Because it is non-returnable loss. While you can make more money in the future, even if you don't have any yet, you can win back money even if you lost some, you can never make, earn or win back time.

Wasting or spending as an attribute doesn't only apply to money, but to time, as well. Time ownership is the ultimate manifestation of Marxism, we all have twenty-four hours a day equally. The problem is that none of us knows how many times twenty-four hours we have left.

In some aspects, wasting time is more costly than wasting money.

We live in an interesting maze: we trade our time for money, so later we can trade our money for time. Most of the time we do both simultaneously. Therefore, we should simultaneously budget our time, as well, not just money.

How do you budget your time?

Just as you do with your money. Have different categories of spending time.

   - The essentials from time's point of view are going to work and satisfying your basic needs.

   - The personal category would stand for your hobbies, human relationships and every other activity that is not essential.

   - The savings would be the time saved for sleeping. (Sleeping can also be considered an essential, but since you can't save up time as you save money, I'd consider sleeping that third wheel in time management that should be scheduled but doesn't fit in the other active categories.)

In time's case the only budget you can make is a daily budget. You have twenty-four units, capital – call them whatever you want. You start each day with the same amount of capital. First think about your daily routines. What do you usually spend time on? Take a piece of paper and write them down.

- Getting ready in the morning.
- Eating once, twice, or three times a day.
- Working X hours.
- Meeting friends.
- Doing chores.
- Other obligations.

After you've listed everything you usually do in a day, try to estimate how much time you spend on each of them. Be real – if you usually spend thirty minutes to get ready in the morning, or you spend an hour consuming your supper, put that on your paper. The point of this exercise is to show you how much time you actually spend on your daily activities, not how much you'd like to. That's the next exercise. When you're finished estimating how much time is spent on your common daily routines, add together those hours and take them as a base for evaluation.

Are you satisfied with what you see? Would you like to have more time for something else? Do you get enough sleep? If the answer is no to any of these questions, it means that you should budget your time better. If you're handling your time wastefully, it is time to figure out a way to fix it.

First clearly define what you would like to have more time for. Then estimate how much time that action would require. Maybe you'd like to spend more time with your parents. What does more mean? Two hours? Three hours? Know what you want and how long would that take, then start fishing for time to jam it into your schedule.

When you know what you want and how many hours that requires, take a look at the paper where you estimated all your activities. Where can you cut a little time? Do you really need forty minutes to get ready in the morning? You can try to do it in twenty. What about lunch? If you sacrifice forty minutes of your lunch time, together with the spared time in the morning, you have already won an extra hour. I don't mean to suggest that you should choke on your lunch. But you have to make priorities: parents or long lunch?

There are activities that sometimes might be helpful and relaxing, but practicing them in an exaggerated manner are the most expensive in time. These are TV, video games, getting lost online shopping. If these things add value to your life, do them. If you're looking for extra time, these are the least risky to resign.

Regardless of what you do, at the end of the day your twenty-four credits will run out. You pay the same amount of time credit for something amazing, challenging and uplifting and something dull and useless. The choice is yours.

In some time budgets this is cool – you can't complain that you're limited in money, because time is neutral in this regard. Surely, if the exciting thing costs a lot of money, you may not be able to pay for it. Yet there are always cheaper excitements out there that are better than watching TV. Everything is a choice. When you choose to play a game for four hours, that's a choice you make sending the message that playing that game is the best way you can spend your time. That is the most valuable activity for those hours. (It can be if you just want to relax and chill out for a few hours after a difficult period, but this is very rarely the case.) Whatever you choose to do in practice becomes more important than any other you could do right in those moments.

The first way to win time is to take a look on your daily activities, and find some minutes here are there. Add these minutes up to win time.

The second way to win time is shortening on purpose gaming, TV and unproductive internet browsing.

The third way to win time is simple, occasional self-reflection: "Is this the best thing I could spend my time on?" Ask yourself this question in random times. If your answer is no, stop what you're doing right away, and meditate a bit on where and how can you improve your time. This exercise is more applicable to the personal time budget category than the essentials. You may conclude that filling out boring forms at your workplace is not the best use of your time, but work has to be done. However, if you catch yourself finding your job an incredibly dull use of time very often, you should consider switching it to something that feels more useful.

To have a proper time budget, build a template on how you can save time. On a different sheet of paper, put down these categories: *must be dones, time wasters, changes I wish to make*. Fill these in each morning. It is almost the same method as the classic "top three priorities checklist" but a bit more complex. The must be dones are the top priorities, but you'll expand this day planner with a list of your personal wishes and add a not-to-do list.

I used to be a huge internet mole. I got distracted a zillion times in different pits of the online prison. Typing letters "FA" and enter was such a reflex action I didn't even notice. When I found myself behind my schedule three months in a row, I decided that some changes needed to be made. I downloaded two apps on my computer, one called Rescue Time and another called Self-Control.

Rescue Time is a smart little app that counts your time spent on each online and offline platform on your computer. When you start using this app, you have to set goals you want to accomplish in doing and not doing. What does this mean? I set that I wanted to spend a total five hours on business, educational and creative sites. I also set that I didn't want to spend more than one hour on shopping, social media and audio-visual sites (namely YouTube, Netflix and the gang). At the end of the day I would get a report from Rescue Time showing me the cruel numbers: did I accomplish my to-do goals, the five hour business, education and creativity? Did I stay within the one-hour frame with the other ones? It is a very good black mirror to check.

The Rescue Time app by itself won't help chronic internet users. You get your report where it says you spent four hours on Amazon and Netflix, and only two on your actual goals. You might get frustrated, pissed or sad, but there is nothing that can prevent you from doing the same thing again the next day. This is where the Self Control app comes into the picture. With this app you can block sites for a few minutes up to twenty-four hours from your browsers. The scariest thing is that you can't overwrite your commands. You can't put Facebook on a ten-hour ban, but lift the ban after two hours because your fingers on your left hand are itching. Once you're out, you're out for good. Amazing! I will donate for this app! Facebook, Twitter, YouTube, Amazon, AliExpress, Sephora, Netflix banned! Boom! I save hours of my life thanks to this one app. By my own experience I'd recommend you using it with moderation, meaning, don't block yourself out for the entire day from your favorite toxic websites. Do two-to-three hour rounds. This way you'll get two to three hours of productivity, but you can have a few minutes to chill between the blocks. Otherwise, you'll just stop using the app, or you'll look for small windows to cheat, like browsing on your phone.

These two apps skyrocketed my productivity and saved me a lot of time. I can highly recommend them. They are free, easy to use and very helpful.

Chapter 8 - Goals For a SMART Budget

SMART Goals

What are your goals? If I woke you up from a deep sleep could you tell them? If not, you have to work on this. The first step in creating a good budget is to know your goals. These goals have to be money related. Personality goals like becoming more patient don't apply here. But if you'd take a paid mindfulness course that helps you with your impatience problem, that applies.

What are your financial goals? Do you want to accumulate savings for a car, house or just in general? Do you have any debts to pay off? If you're just about to start college and undertaking a cartload of debt, what would you want to do in college to minimize the debt by the time you finish it?

Budgeting is not easy. It involves painful compromises, difficult choices, and many renunciations. Still, having a goal, something that holds the promise of all your sacrifices being worthy, it will make budgeting seem less painful. You plan and save for your future and present wellbeing.

The best way to set financial goals is to follow the SMART goal technique. SMART is an abbreviation for Specific, Measurable, Achievable, Relevant, and Time-framed.

Financial goals, just like any other goal, can be divided in two or three time categories: short term, long term and optionally mid-term. Short term is a time frame between a few months up to a year. Long term is three to five to ten year plans. Mid-term goals therefore stand for plans that need more than one but less than three years to be realized.

For example, let's say that you want to go on a vacation to Fiji when you reach the first monthly 20,000 dollars in income to celebrate your achievement. However, based on your calculations, this won't happen in the next two years. This forecasting makes the Fiji trip a mid-term goal. You have twenty-four months to save money for it. After some research you calculated that the trip to Fiji would be somewhere around 6,000 dollars. 6,000 divided by 24 is 250. This is the amount you have to save monthly for your dream trip to Fiji. In a nutshell, this is how a SMART goal looks like.

It is specific: you plan on doing the trip after you reach your 20,000 dollar monthly income goal to celebrate your accomplishment. The goal is also measurable, it's 6,000 dollars. It is achievable since you know you need to save 250 dollars each month. It is your dream trip as a self-reward, therefore it is relevant to you. It also has a time-frame, namely two years.

(The numbers and the example are just for the argument's sake. I didn't do any research on how much a trip to Fiji is, so don't take the 6,000 dollars for granted.)

Where is Your Money Coming From?

Knowing your SMART goals is only the first step in smart budgeting. You have to dig deeper into your financial reality. Collect all your income sources. Make a list of them: work, loans, royalties, parents, interest payments, etc. Add an amount, or an estimate amount, to each source. I suggest doing it in a monthly distribution. (If you have 100,000 dollars in a bank that brings you three percent interest each year do the following: 100,000 x 3% = 3000. 3000/12 = 250. This means you have to write 250 dollars on your monthly interest income. It is a simplistic example, I didn't consider yearly handling charges and other fees.)

If you can't know for sure how much income you'll have from a source, like royalties, estimate an average based on the real data of the past three months, and extract one third of the average. You won't find this method in any economic or finance book. This is just me counting for a worst-case scenario. Nevertheless, it works. Usually the worst-case estimate is not correct, but I forecast my budget with those numbers. This way I never exceed my budget.

For example I made 80, 120 and 100 dollars in the past three months. The calculation I have to make is a simple average counting:

$(80+120+100)/3 = 300/3 = 100$

This means that my average income of the past three months is 100 dollars. But this is not bad enough. I need to extract 1/3 from this number. One third of one hundred is:

$100/3 = 33.3$

Now I know what to extract:

$100-33.3=66.7$

Long story short, my pessimist estimate budget for the next month is 67 dollars. It is significantly less than my worst month from the three examined, but this way the risks are low for any negative surprise. When estimating money income, I think it is always better to expect the worst and hope for the best.

Where is your money going?

After you check where your money comes from, take a look at where your money goes. My five-category budgeting is a very good, transparent way of tracking where your money flows. Before you can make a budget forecast and plan for longer term, you have to know how you're spending your money. Use an Excel chart to record and track on what and how much money you spend.

Don't forget to categorize your expenses. You don't have to do it with the same categories I did. You can simply go with the essentials-savings-personal category trio from Mint method. Or you can have fixed-variable-nonessential expenses. Here, fixed means monthly recurring checks and bills. Variable means expenses where price is not predictable, like gas expense, or food. Nonessential stands for everything else, like pleasure expenses. This transparent record tracking is the shortest and easiest way to know where can you cut and reform your spending.

Be Flexible

Don't stick to your budgeting plans if you notice a

better way to do it, or if you find it hard to follow. For example, if you notice another place where you can cut, or you wish to regroup your resources because your priorities changed, or you can't save as much as you planned without lacking in essentials, you need to reframe the budget.

You need a new strategy for controlling your costs if you exceed your budget. In this case, always start your revision with the personal, nonessential, Clothes and Makeup category – regardless of how you call it. A little shirt here, another night out there, and those bucks are flying out your wallet. As I said in the previous chapters, it is very helpful to set a cap on these expenses. To make the caps more illustrative, divide the number into a per day cost. For example, if you have one hundred dollars set for entertainment per month, it would be 3.3 dollars per day. A cinema ticket is somewhere among twelve to sixteen dollars. If you go out to a movie, know that you spent your daily entertainment budget for three to five days in advance.

If you can't cut enough from your personal cost category in order to balance your budget, you will need to touch your essential and saving categories. Choose a cheaper phone and internet plan, move to a cheaper flat, sell your car, put your retirement account on hold for a month, you name it. One thing is sure. If you have a hundred dollars for your disposal, you can't spend a hundred and one without entering in debt. To avoid it and save something, don't spend more than ninety-nine dollars.

Chapter 9 – Budget, Thrive and Be Happy

Budgeting Boosts Self-Confidence and Self-Worth

Budgeting develops several virtues, like frugality, resilience, willpower, self-control and ultimately self-esteem and confidence. If you say no to something that you want, even if you could afford it, it will boost your self-worth. You just made a sensible, rational decision, respected your money and avoided spending on clutter. The more often you say no, and the longer term you keep your budget in the black, the more confident you'll become in your willpower, good judgment, reasonable mentality and self-control.

Saying no is an essential skill in business and personal life. You'll never please everybody. If you never say no, you'll have less and less time to do things that matter to you. People will also take advantage – consciously or unconsciously – of you, being the yes man. Practicing and developing a strong sense of saying no for yourself will ultimately help you to say no to others. It will result in more you-time. You'll be able to devote time to your own wishes and needs. Saying no without self-doubt is the sign of a strong, self-aware character. Saying no is part of being more assertive. If you cannot learn to say no, you'll face many frustrations and stresses in your life.

It is admirable helping others, but if you do it against your interest, you'll make your needs inferior to others'. This is where low self esteem and low self-respect roots. Put an end to this and learn to be more assertive. If you can't start with others, practice saying no to your budget. You'll feel an empowering difference. "If I said no to myself, no way I'll say yes to X,Y,Z."

Budget for Experiences

A well-designed budget can actually make you spend more on the things that make you the happiest. Budgeting doesn't always have to mean spending less, but even if it does, spending smarter can end up making you happier. If you don't buy ten valueless items, and only three of important value, you'll feel much happier.

How can budgeting be directly related to happiness? Matt J. Goren, professor at the University of Georgia, says that if you focus your financial resources on things that directly improve your life, you'll feel happier for two reasons. The first reason is the obvious: you'll add real value to your life. The other reason is the feeling you'll get by spending less for a better value.

Meeting minimum needs is essential for happiness. This is true in the case of each budgeting category: essentials, savings and personal. Don't misunderstand what high quality life means to you. It might not necessarily mean paying a high mortgage on a newly built, extravagant house or a posh car. While these may be important, they are not essential to live a happy, high quality life. The happiness they provide runs out very quickly. Then, only the pain of the mortgage remains, and the trap of a high cash flow demand to pay it off. Long term luxuries that require long-term, high-cost commitment actually make you more depressed and stressed.

The same rules apply to any habitual "hedonic treadmill" purchases like a two-hundred-channel cable TV package, the newest smartphone, or home delivery food service. After a short while they won't be special anymore. We'll take them for granted, and they'll inevitably fade into the greyness of habit. Not so with the recurring monthly expense they require.

On the other hand, each one-time unique purchase will offer a fresh happiness boost. The better value and shorter-term money commitment it requires, the better. By reducing the hedonic treadmill costs in favor of new experiences, we'll feel a profound joy in life.

Paying for experiences always pays off better in your memory as happiness – as opposed to momentary satisfaction. Some think that paying for a brief moment in time would be less of a good deal than buying something that lasts for months or years. However, studies have proved that we actually enjoy experiences more than material things when it comes to spending. Why? Firstly, because positive feelings start to accumulate when we start anticipating the event. It lasts through the event and even after it.

There's a reason why start-ups like Airbnb thrive. They offer an experience instead a layover. The Apple Company tries the same thing with its products by transforming their ownership into an experience, instead of just having a phone.

New stuff sooner or later becomes old stuff. Sometimes, even before they become old stuff, the "value" bar raises making them uncool. If the Joneses get a better model of that object, what you just bought could be devalued. Even if we're the Joneses, the joy felt by the purchase will slowly decrease by day.

Joy felt through experience, on the other hand, can stay with you for a lifetime. The first night spent in a tent, the first skydiving jump, or seeing the ocean for the first time give such profound positive feelings that no object can overwrite. Experiences ultimately become part of your identity. Objects serve as an external mask, but they won't define you. Experiences, however, become one with your soul through internal processing, through the stories you tell by going through your value filter and lifting your self-esteem. Many people have climbed a mountain, but no one did it like you. No one felt the same things as you did. It's your unique, individual story. It's you. You won't feel the need to keep up with the Joneses either when it comes to subjective experiencing. Emotions and feelings can't be quantified.

Experiences can't be taken for granted and never become a routine. They are fleeting. This gives them even more value.

Live, thrive, experience. Budgeting to go camp for only one night in your surroundings costs just as much as an expensive dinner you'll eat in a few minutes. If you spend an amount anyway, make the money worth a life-time.

Chapter 10 -Small Budgeting Tips

As someone who used to live on a less than two hundred dollars a month for half a decade, I could fill an entire book with budgeting tips. Maybe one day I will. For now, I collected my and others' fifty best budgeting tips and tricks.

1. Cook at home a large meal that doesn't spoil quickly. I used to do a huge bowl of tomato, mushroom, and ham pasta with cheese. I always put the cheese on at the end, after warming up a portion. It was delicious and filling. I used to eat it for three, even four days a row in times of scarcity.

2. Bring your lunch to work, or school.

3. Avoid buying snacks at your workplace's or school's buffet. They are always more

pricey than buying them at your local grocery store.

4. Prepare your coffee at home. A box of instant coffee enough for 120 cups usually starts at $6.99 at Safeway. True, it's not the best quality, but desperate times call for desperate measures. Imagine how much money would you save on 120 Tall Caramel Lattes. Don't imagine: I calculated it for you, including the cost of the SafeWay coffee: ($4 x 120) − $6.99 = $473.01. Multiply this number with 3, and you'll get your annual savings just on coffee.

5. Never go grocery shopping when you're hungry. I think everybody knows what I mean.

6. Prepare a strict list before you go grocery shopping. When you enter the store, go directly to get the products on your list. Beware the red and yellow sales boards unless the product you want to purchase can be bought for less.

7. Buy bulk deals from the products you consume often.

8. Trade fancy brands for generic ones. I honestly like some Walgreens products more than the original, higher-priced version. If you check the ingredients sometimes, you can be surprised that the generic version has more nutrients and less carbs than the main one.

9. Reuse grocery bags. Even better, get some canvas or cloth bags that last longer.

10. If you happen to buy bags at the grocery store, use them as garbage bags.

11. Pay your bills first thing to avoid late payment fees.

12. Consolidate your debt repayment on an interest rate as small as possible. Interest is money you never spent and never enjoyed. Try to minimize it as much as you can.

13. Avoid credit cards with annual fees.

14. Don't have multiple phone lines. Strive to have only one good, cover-all package. Discard your landline.

15. Buy used books or borrow them from libraries.

16. Bottle your water.

17. Try to keep your things as long as possible. You don't need to buy a new fridge if the repair is easy and cheap. You don't need a new car every two, five or even ten years. Until repair bills don't exceed prepayment fees, you're fine with the good old Mustang. Don't skip regular maintenance checks. Bills can be much friendlier if the car gets fixed before their wheels fall off.

18. Do Uber pool.

19. Ride a bike, or walk as often as you can.

20. If you eat out, do it during happy hour.

21. Choose early movies at the movie theater instead of the evening ones. Tickets can be up to fifty percent cheaper.

22. Unplug your electric appliances when you don't use them.

23. Plan vacations or major spending, like a refurbishment or a new phone, ahead of time.

24. Set up automatic savings.

25. Put a big part of your work bonus, inheritance, or tax refund into your savings account.

26. Save your loose change. Collect it until the end of the year and treat yourself with something from it. You'll be surprised how much money will add up.

27. Switch your value analysis from price –cost to working hours – value. Something might not seem worthless if you look at the price. But, if you calculate how many hours

you worked for that thing, you might change your mind about the purchase.

28. Unsubscribe from sales newsletters, especially from those products that are expensive even when discounted.

29. Set your bill payment on auto-pay. On one hand, this saves you from unwanted delay fees. On the other hand, some providers offer a minor discount if you choose auto-pay.

30. Pay off your credit cards in full each month. Don't buy the miles and cash back fairy dust. They won't help you if you fall into debt.

31. Set gift price limits among your family and friends. No expensive birthday or Christmas gifts. Handmade, heartfelt stuff prevail.

32. Don't buy cheap or discounted stuff just because it's cheap.

33. Trade things within family. Maybe you have an extra TV and your aunt has an extra couch. Trade them if demand asks it. This way it will be a win-win.

34. When it comes to easy house refurbishments, ask your friends for help. Pledge to help too if your friends need it.

35. Have a "no spend" day, let's say right after the day you cooked a meal big enough for multiple days.

36. Waterproof your home. It's easier and less costly to fix a small hole than an entire roof.

37. Keep the sun out in summer. Instead of going crazy on air conditioning, get reflective curtains that keep the heat out.

38. Use less water.

39. Switch off the lights after you leave a room.

40. Invest more time to find the best low airfare deals.

41. If you keep your money in cash at home, put the monthly amount in an envelope for each budgeting category. This way you'll know that when the "personal" envelope gets empty, you're done spending in that category.

42. Compare your insurance yearly before renewing. In a year there might be a better deal on the market.

43. Winterize your home. Before it gets foggy and frosty, make sure that your home is properly insulated. When heating bills are as high as they are, you shouldn't pay on heating the entire cosmos. Repair and prepare for winter.

44. Buy warm water bottles and use those as heaters instead of an extra radiator on full power. You can buy water bottles with sweet knit covers for as much as five dollars. Before you get too cozy, do a

safety check to see if they leak, and don't use warmer water than the indicated.

45. Dress up. Another typical winter mistake people do is that they try to wear their summer clothes at home in winter, as well heating the house up to summer heat. Don't do that. Dress up accordingly to the season at home, too.

46. If you can afford the installment, use a programmable thermostat.

47. Check for free events. I just booked a free Tim Ferriss event in San Francisco. Check the schedule of the apps Eventbrite and Meetup and snap up the best free events in town.

48. Pair up with friends and family when buying Netflix, Spotify or other services. You can add up to five people in your package, and you can also divide the costs among them.

49. Use Uber instead of taxis, use Airbnb instead of hotels, and check Tripadvisor for the best meal deals when you travel.

50. Buy summer clothes in winter and winter clothes in summer. This way you'll find them on a fifty to seventy percent discount.

+1: Avoid shopping with people who have excessive spending habits. Shopping frenzy is captivating and addicting. Before you know it, you will also leave Macy's with two handfuls of bags and your personal spending is spent for six months. Don't forget, you can always return full priced or slightly discounted items.

Final Words

Budgeting is not a habit but a lifestyle. As I mentioned in the beginning of this book, pairing budgeting lifestyle change with the adoption of minimalism can be a stylish yet cost efficient solution.

I directed the content of the book to those who need to budget because they are needy. If you happen to be well off, it doesn't mean you don't have to or you can't budget. By now, you must know that budgeting is much more than just saving money. It is:

- a way to improve willpower and self-esteem
- the method to spend on things that make you happy vs. valueless mess
- planning out life-long lasting positive memories by experiences

- keeping a financial system
- making your spending more transparent and relevant
- learning to improve your relationship with money
- learning to improve your self-image
- gathering financial knowledge
- saving money proportionally to your income
- having peace of mind.

Budgeting can make your life so much easier with very little effort. I hope I could prove it to you and make you excited about budgeting. Trust your judgment, and if you truly commit, you'll become an excellent minimalist on a budget.

I believe in you!

Zoe

P.S.: If you have questions please don't hesitate to contact me on **zoemckey@gmail.com**. I welcome any kind of constructive opinion as well. I'd like to know how I can help so please share your ideas with me. If you'd like to get helpful tips from me on a weekly basis, visit me at **www.zoemckey.com** and subscribe. Thank you!

More Books By Zoe

Build Grit

Find What You Were Born For – Book 1

Find What You Were Born For – Book 2

Find Who You Were Born To Be

Catching Courage

Fearless

Daily Routine Makeover

Daily Routine Makeover – Morning Edition

Daily Routine Makeover – Evening Edition

Less Mess Less Stress

Braver Than You Believe

The Unlimited Mind

Wired For Confidence

Minimalist Makeover

Build Social Confidence

Communication and Confidence Coaching

By working with me you can expect to gain a better understanding of yourself, and the hope you need to change your life for the better. I will help you understand everybody around you better starting with yourself. My three main goals are to help you:

- Embrace discomfort to break down your negative beliefs,

- Find your strengths and focus on them,

- Bring out the side of you that is totally comfortable with yourself and your environment.

I have a unique approach to coaching. The entire lesson is composed of two parts:

143

Interpersonal Skills Development

Do your palms sweat and your heart pound when you enter in a room full of strangers? Do you feel awkward when somebody starts a conversation with you? Do you fear you'll run out of things to say and wish you could just talk casually with everybody?

Then this course was made for you!

In this section, I'll help you learn how to communicate with others, how to be presentable, and how to always make a great impression. Humans are social beings and since you live among them you can never underestimate the importance of social skills. If you have them you can be 100-percent present and aware in any situation. I have been studying and developing communication and real-life social interaction skills for more than 10 years. I've written 10 books – all of them Amazon best-sellers – on the topic. I can help you, please let me!

Here you will learn:

• How to start conversations and keep them going with anybody,

• How to "win friends and influence people,"

• Airy, pleasant ways to be more charming and likable,

• How to be the life of the party, and

• Tips on how to handle difficult conversations and people.

I'll teach you how to be the person everyone notices when you enter the room, the person who instantly sparks people's interest and can talk easily to anyone.

Intrapersonal Skills Development

Is the mirror your worst enemy? Or the scale? Or both? Do you feel uncomfortable with who you are? Do you sometimes feel your days are passing by without any purpose? Is sleeping your favorite activity? Do you wish you were somewhere else, maybe someone else?

If any of these statements apply to you then you have work to do. Living with self-contempt, regrets, and frustration is not sustainable. In this part of the coaching I will help you to accept and recover from any inner struggles you have. With honesty and commitment, I will guide you to let go of old wounds, and help you find your strengths and develop them in order to bring out the best in yourself.

I'll help you:

- to discover the root cause of your problems,
- recover from childhood traumas,
- communicate with yourself objectively and silence the malicious voices in your head,
- build confidence and self-respect, and learn to be persistent and get what you want.

If you're interested, apply here:

http://www.zoemckey.com/contact/

Made in the USA
San Bernardino, CA
16 June 2017